Where in the World We Meet

Poems

Todd Outcalt

Chatter House Press
Indianapolis

Where in the World We Meet
Poems

Copyright © 2014 by Todd Outcalt

For information:

Chatter House Press
7915 S Emerson Ave, Ste B303
Indianapolis, IN 46237

chatterhousepress.com

ISBN: 978-1-937793-21-0
Library of Congress Control Number: 2014936117

Also by Chatter House Press

beyond first words
Penny Dunning

Street Girls Have Guns
Gregg DeBoor

Battle Scarred
Jason Ammermon

Almost Music From Between Places
Steven R. Roberts

Some Poems To Be Read Out Loud
Richard Pflum

Muntu Kuntu Energy
Mwatabu Okantah

World of Mortal Light
Virginia Slachman

Hot Type Cold Read
Tony Brewer

Written in the Dish Pit
Adam Henze

Inside Virgil's Garage
Lindsey Martin-Bowen

For Becky

All the world's a stage,
and all the men and women merely players.

Shakespeare, As You Like It

Acknowledgments

I would like to thank Penny Dunning for seeing the value in my poetry, for holding out the promise of this, my first collection, and for subsequently providing the opportunity for me to bring together both early and more current work.

I also thank the editors of the various magazines and journals in which many of these poems first appeared—some in different forms. And I give grateful acknowledgment to the following publications:

Christmas Lights (a CD): "Christmas Lights"

Husband's Guide to Breast Cancer: "The Explorer Turns Toward Home"

Loch Raven Review: "The Pileated Woodpecker"

Rattle: "On the First Anniversary of His Wife's Death"

Satire and Comment: "Midas Touch", "One Percent", "The Death of the Wall Street Trader"

Still Point Arts Quarterly: "American Gothic, by Grant Wood"

The Barefoot Review: "Breast Implants", "Scars"

The Christian Century: "Advent" © *The Christian Century*, "Advent" is reprinted by permission of *The Christian Century*, originally published in issue December 12, 2010

The Christian Science Monitor: "Black Holes", "Shelf Life"

The Lyric: "Full Moon", "The Death of the Greek Professor", "Window to the Soul", "Odysseus Meets Tiresias in Hades"

The New Poet: "Scarecrow"

The Oklahoma Review: "Manche El Baile En San Juan"

The Road Less Taken: "On My Daughter's Wedding Day", "The Snowman in Summer", "Home From Rugby Practice", "Jesus Boy"

The Upper Room: "Time Was"

Together: "Today I Shall Sit in Silence"

Wellspring: "Jerald" (Originally titled "Re-Insurrection")

Writers' Journal: "Punctuation"

Introduction

Unlike my work in prose—particularly fiction, essays and the ever-looming deadlines of books—my poetry has sandwiched the adolescent and latter years of my life. I began writing poetry in the late 1970s as a high school student, continued through college, and even produced some published verse that provided the occasion for a nice meal or a celebration with friends. In those days I also eagerly read in coffeehouses and those smoke-filled bars that provided open-mic opportunities for poets and singers. My hair and beard were long and my verse oscillated between the deadly-serious and the indelibly-light.

But as my attentions turned toward marriage, children, and forging a domestic balance of work and family, I gravitated toward those longer forms—particularly books—that could provide me a contract and consequently the hope of, even if meager, royalty. Poetry was shoved backstage, hidden behind the brighter flats of pastoral ministry, of agents and publishers—save for the occasional piece of light verse I wrote for birthdays, anniversaries or dinner conversation.

Although I was not writing poetry for more than two decades, however, the form was never out of sight or earshot. I continued to read and listen to those poets—both long past and contemporary—who captured my imagination and my ear.

Then, suddenly in 2009, in preparation for a twenty-fifth anniversary Caribbean cruise, I began writing poetry again and discovered a voice—particularly centered in those domestic and romantic pursuits that seemed to border on the confessional. Poets don't need much more—and I am grateful for the sounds and forms that took hold early in the mornings, late at night, or even while driving to an appointment. Such is the power of poetry, and as some of my verse began wresting its way into literary journals and those whimsical publications that appreciated my humor, I found that my voice morphed and adapted toward the periphery of esoteric themes and ideas, if not in classical form.

Even now, I am still trying to capture my voice.

In this collection I have attempted to give some movement and shape to the themes and subject matter, much as I may have experienced or written them in a haphazard life, free from the constraints of order but more accurately defined by chaos and uncertainty.

I thank the reader for taking a chance on an unknown—and hope that these poems can speak to both the particular and the universal as we encounter our world . . . especially in love and laughter.

~T.O.

Table of Contents

LOVE

WHERE IN THE WORLD WE MEET.. 3
FULL MOON 4
WHY THE CLOCK CHIMES 5
YOUNG LOVE 6
HER BUSINESS TRIP 7
THE GIFT.. 8
REFRIGERATOR MAGNETS 9
MANCHE EL BAILE EN SAN JUAN 10
BLACK HOLES 11
TONIGHT.. 12
THE SOMMELIER'S LOVE SONG... 13
AN EVENING ANYWHERE... 14
THE ARCHITECT 15
SKIN-DEEP 16
WEDDING ANNIVERSARY.. 17
THE EXPLORER TURNS TOWARD HOME...................................... 18
SCARS... 19
THE PHYSICIST PROFESSES HIS LOVE IN THE STARS 20
WHAT WE DO NOT SAY WHEN WE SPEAK OF LOVE 21
THE DREAM VOYAGE OF CHRISTOPHER COLUMBUS...................... 22
AUTUMN WALK 23
WE SHALL BE OLD SOMEDAY... 24
AN EVENING SUCH AS THIS.. 25
SHELF LIFE... 26
THE RACONTEUR'S FOOTNOTES.. 27
SOME THOUGHTS ABOUT YOU 28
SONG OF MY (YOUNGER) SELF.. 29
THE SUNDAY AFTERNOON 30
BREAST IMPLANTS... 31
CARIBBEAN CRUISE 32
NOT A LOVE POEM 33
10:00 P.M. 34
DÉJÀ VU 35
EQUATIONS WE HAVE KNOWN 36
THE GRAVITY OF BODIES 38
THIS IS NOT A LOVE POEM... 39

LIFE

Twenty-one 43
Sixteen 44
The Dorm 45
The Graduate 46
Home from Rugby Practice 47
Jesus Boy 48
The Salutatorian 49
Natural Selection 50
The Doppler Effect 51
Greek Grammar Lessons 52
The gods, Retired 53
Autumn Kaleidoscope 54
The Son in the Basement 55
Odysseus Meets Tiresias in Hades 56
Centuries 57
Butcher, Baker 58
Consider the Birds 59
Red Shift 60
An Easter Prayer 61
Milkweed 62
Advent 63
An Advent Prayer 64
The Christ Child's Prayer 65
Superman 66
Redbuds 67
Maundy Thursday 68
Communion 69
Rooms 70
My Mother's Arms 72
My Father's Legs 73
Ideas 74
In Praise of Women 75
Drums 76
Geometry 77
Sunday Morning 78
Autumn 79
Questions in the Night 80
Chemotherapy 81
Houdini Speaks to His Widow 82
On My Daughter's Wedding Day 83
A Prayer on My Daughter's Wedding Day 84
On the First Anniversary of His Wife's Death 85

JERALD... 86
ALTERNATIVE CHRISTMASES.. 87
NATIVITY SOMNAMBULISM... 88
WORLD WITHOUT END... 89
THE ANGEL SPEAKS GLAD TIDINGS TO THE SHEPHERDS 90
CHRISTMAS LIGHTS 91
THE GODDESS OF LITTLE THINGS... 92
WATERING THE ROSES ON A SATURDAY MORNING... 93
INSIDE THIS DAY 94
THREE VERSIONS OF MYSELF.. 95
GOOD FRIDAY, NEW YORK 96
AMERICAN GOTHIC, BY GRANT WOOD 97
II. 98
PORTRAIT OF ELIZABETH I BY NICHOLAS HILLIARD, 1585................................. 98
III. 99
NIGHTHAWKS, BY EDWARD HOPPER.. 99
HORIZON 100
TIME WAS... 101
WHEN WE WERE GODS 102
THE DEATH OF THE GREEK PROFESSOR.. 104
THE SCARECROW 105
THE WORLD PREMIER.. 106
HUMMINGBIRDS... 107
THE GREEK PROFESSOR OFFERS HIS APOLOGY 108
VACANCY 109
THE FATHER CONSIDERS HIS DEPRESSED SON 110
LULLABY... 111
BLESSING 112
THE PILEATED WOODPECKER 113
TODAY I SHALL SIT IN SILENCE 116
WINDOW TO THE SOUL... 117

LIGHT

One Percent 121
Skin 122
Old Golfers... 123
The Death of the Wall Street Trader 124
Punctuation.. 125
Closet 128
The Snowman in Summer 129
Midas Touch 130
To Old Men 131
Fraternity Song 133
You 134
The Old Married Couple Reflects...................... 135
The Luddite.. 136
Origami 138

LOVE

Where in the World We Meet

Somewhere on this measured continent
Perhaps our eyes met on a carousel,
Our longitude's improbable percent
Since solitudes run often parallel.
Drafted by fate, we may have spoken once,
Or nodded in the grace of gratitude,
Or seen each other for some weeks or months
Before life beat us down in latitude
And broke our fall on some remoter world
Where people do not meet by happenstance
Or other possibilities unfurled.
But in this time and place circumferenced
By love I fell for you, as you for me:
Star-crossed, perhaps . . . or just geography.

Full Moon

This moon tonight has never shone before,
Nor cast its light among these darkened trees.
No aid to Homer as he spun his lore
Nor comfort to the death of Socrates.

There was no moon like this among the flowers
Wet with Roman dew, nor when the rain
Blessed multitudes and kept faith in the hours
Before the golden age of Charlemagne.

This moon was kept in secret for tonight,
For such a time as this, where, idly by
We rest inside each other in its light.
And in embrace, we stare into the sky
Which gives no answer, nor asks the neutral night
To tell us this is love, nor reasons why.

Why the Clock Chimes

Some nights when we are home alone, and time
Slips past our ears like fast years flung
Into our years like participles, I dream you young
Again, and wish that I were in my prime.
I would go back and give my life to you
When our first hope was fastened on such days
As these, and deny how the past outweighs
The future as though our love were new.
I would not give small portions of my years,
Nor hold you less as evening chimes—our lives doled
Out in occupations, our kids grown old—
But cherish you as each new minute nears.
I would not be time's tersest guardian,
But in these fleeting seconds love you once again.

Young Love

I saw the two, their hands entwined,
Strolling down the coffee avenue,
And realized that we had passed that way,
As we were young once, too.

I watched them bound across the street,
Their laughter lilting higher in the air,
And hoped that I had been as sharp as he
Or half as debonair.

And when they disappeared in run
My mind was hurried toward a rendezvous
When life was fresh and bleached with summer sun
And I had first met you.

Her Business Trip

After years of nightly necking,
Conversations at the sink,
Brushing, flossing, and spot-checking,
I am fonder than I think

Of noting your nuances late
At night, or hurried to the bed
Where we might pause to contemplate
The words we could have said.

And I, without these rituals,
Can hardly stand the thought of me,
Alone among residuals
Of your absentee

Smile and movements as you turn
Into the crowd and say goodbye.
Words fail, waiting for your return:
Thought I should clarify.

The Gift

I make you a gift of this irretrievable day
Beneath the sun's stare, a blink of cloud,
The evening's bed pulled back like a shroud.

And what is more, I shall not presume to say
A word since words may consequently fall
Headlong into meaning or mean nothing at all.

Refrigerator Magnets

Clinging to the stainless steel
Sides of my refrigerator
The magnets congregate, congeal
In herds of calendars, or

Friends who love their photos taken.
And here, my wife sticks odd reminders
Of recipes that I'm to bake in
The oven. My children paste rejoinders

To questions I had posed so long ago
My memory has faded, and all
We share are pizza hotlines and so
Many numbers we don't call.

The coupons hang like flat bananas
In bunches long ago expired,
And concert tickets that my son has
Purchased clutch the steel like tired

Chaperones on boring dates.
And on the tiny blackboard, see—
My wife sends love and contemplates
The strength of our polarity.

Manche El Baile En San Juan

That night, waltzing the streets of old San Juan,
A quarter century of marriage made—
The walls of *Fuerte San Felipe del Morro*
Embracing our joy, our history's strong defense—
We jazzed, and loved, and drank our silver toast
Beneath the arms of *Paseo la Princesa,*
Still dreaming of the years ahead and time
Together dancing into *dulce amor.*

Those songs—yearning, rhythmic, sorrowful—
Sang our lovely history, years, and sex
Borne on hardwood waves of salsa dusk.
Samba, sarabande, rumba, twist:
We tangoed into the night's sweet sweat
And kissed the heat still rising between us.

Black Holes

There are points in space
Consuming light and matter:
Dark places science cannot explain
Where galaxies, like a double-helix ladder,
Empty to a pull like a drain.

And in the infinitesimal cosmos
Of the heart, which Einstein proved
Is not the shortest distance of a straight line,
You are the point toward which my world has moved . . .
Just in the nick of time.

Tonight

I have decided to love you tonight.
The children are asleep, the dishes dirty,
The glasses empty of ice,
And in this silence I have made my choice
To love you again, to open my hands,
To withhold nothing from you.
Let us forget the misery and despair
Of the world, our work and stress,
And for tonight embrace
The comfort of each other.
I wish to discover
Some secret corner of your soul
Where your pain and heartache hides
And where our love,
Unspoken, unashamed,
Resides.

The Sommelier's Love Song

These empty stems will soon be filled
With Zinfandel or Chardonnay—
Tart, white sweetness, slightly chilled,
Sipped at the close of day.

The dryness of the Cabernet
Will serve as prelude, deep and red,
To passions bold through their bouquet
And cellared in our bed.

An Evening Anywhere

She was there first, singing her all,
And he came later like a waterfall
Spilling over her precipice from a great height.
Her legs wrapped his limp body like a pall.
And it was night.

The Architect

How long before these stones were cut and timber hewn
Had I drawn plans to build the perfect life?
Long before I bought this site, or you my wife
Reviewed the blueprints, or the survey strewn

Over the firm foundations of time,
Or hands that once were strong began to tremble
In the wilt of weakness, and feeble
Compromises claimed what once was mine.

How many years have slipped through compass come,
Or progress stalled, and crumbled in these walls,
Before I built a place for you in narrow halls
And carried you over thresholds, rejoicing, when I brought you home?

Skin-Deep

In the wet circle of a downtown day
I saw you exiting with several friends
The lively circus of the tapas bar.

And for a moment I was swept away
Into the secret corners of our life
Where we have loved and drank our reservoir.

And as I stepped into the casual
Greetings and the rote familiar word
I thought I glimpsed acknowledgment in you:

The way you smiled, or nodded not at all,
That made me think it was your voice I heard,
Or that you loved me more than when I knew

That we would finish one another's thought,
Or mark the routine hours with long days, like air,
When nothing quite remarkable, just sleep,

Would pass between us, or we had forgot
To say "I love you", as we might a prayer,
Standing in the rain—like this—skin deep.

Wedding Anniversary

I will not remember this day a hundred years from now
After our sun has set, or the moon slipped inside
The dark pouch of the pines.

Nothing will keep me from forgetting how we lived
Through a breviary of days, solid with the tedious
Tasks which carried us through time.

Nor will I recall as men cannot the reasons why we loved
As lovers do, long after our song has ceased
Its rhythm and rhyme.

All that I know is that we sung best what we sung
When songs were no longer young
And none were yours or mine.

The Explorer Turns Toward Home

I have sailed vast seas in search of you
And slogged through jungles dark with poison vine,
Charted the far lands of Timbuktu
While tortured by the fly and porcupine.
I have dodged pits and hungry cannibals,
Persevered through sleet and spitting snow,
Oared down rivers, survived waterfalls
And mutinous friends who craved the status-quo.
And I have seen the end of earth and time:
Unknown cultures, forests, desert plains,
Azure cities, mountains I could not climb,
Such beauties now but where your heart remains.
But as I turn toward home my sustenance
Is you, and I desire your face above these continents.

Scars

Show me your scars and I'll show you mine:
Your scalpels drawn through healthy flesh,
Your broken half and half as more removed,
And deeper cuts where mine remain unseen.

We heal each other in these tender wounds,
Each sorrow shared, each bone our bone,
Embracing what we cannot speak in sounds
And naming what we dare not speak alone.

The Physicist Professes His Love in the Stars

I spoke, and from deep light learned to exist.
But time—this brief affair, this lonely prism—
Confirmed that love was years, a solipsism
Of unproved theory, and I, love's physicist.

What We Do Not Say When We Speak of Love

When I met you with your friends
I feigned to say "I love you" in the worst way,
But I am not given to public displays of affection
Or to romantic ends of chance.

And so I smiled and nodded—
A hint you understood with an affirming glance
As we might choose to reminisce
What sign you are, or fingerprint,
Or even if you steal my love without a kiss,
You know exactly what I meant.

The Dream Voyage of Christopher Columbus

I have sailed for you over familiar waters,
Night's tranquility and days deep blue,
Sunlight spread like a pall over the slick decks
Hastening our rendezvous.

And I have glimpsed green lands plush with fruit
Lost in these wonders taciturn,
Pressing toward home through uncharted waters
And the point of no return.

Autumn Walk

I follow you through the confluence of fields
Plodding over the bent stalks where
The harvest has reaped the sun's fruit
      Out of thin air

And in this quiet moment where
We have come from or are going
I sense that I discover you here
      Though not knowing

If we shall reach the sunlight
A half mile up the narrow pass
Or if we should make our morning here
      In the soft grass

We Shall Be Old Someday

We shall be old someday when the children are grown,
When the house is silent, the attic spare . . .
And then I will find you everywhere.

We shall be old someday with our photos faded,
Our passions quenched by a coffee thirst . . .
And I will love you as at the first.

We shall be old someday when the evening is dark,
When our teeth are false, our opinions honest . . .
And I will love you as I promised.

We shall be old someday with a pension plan,
The mortgage paid, our work at end . . .
And then we shall be young again.

An Evening Such as This

To K.M.

What shall we say to each other on an evening such as this?
Embraced by the verisimilitudes of all
That we have known and built in our life's call,
The pendulum pull of quiet moments we shall miss?
What magnanimous artifacts can we unearth
After all these years of unwavering love,
Displayed on shelves, and identified in a lifetime of
Soliloquies we have spoken? And what new birth
Awaits us in the days ahead, where we can't see
Beyond what we have known, but have hoped for, nonetheless?
Tonight, let us find peace in each other, and quietly express
What we do not need to say. Let us agree
That love will see us through when life is rough,
And our sight dim, and these words are not enough.

Shelf Life

I can read you like a book:
Your loved and lovely lines
Your well-thumbed pages
Your knowing-look
The shape of your spine.

And I have held you in such times
When light was dim
And truth absurd
Knowing I could turn your page
And read
Beginning to end
What I could not gauge
Nor comprehend.

The Raconteur's Footnotes

Those years when we were young and free
Were not the best years of our lives.
As I recall, decidedly,
Extremes were often wrapped around
Some pleasant memory [1]

Subdued by worry, shot with stress,
Or bent by money's paperweight,
We forged ahead. Our stalled progress
Semantics could not calculate
Through our forgetfulness.

The children ate our savings, drank
Our love, consumed our energies. [2]
And by the time we checked the bank
Our short assets were seized
And our years in the tank.

You may have thought I did not note
The subtleties of certain days: [3]
Your changing face, your overcoat,
Or expressed love through time's essays
Before words seized my throat.

But I remember more than these [4]
That feigned illusions in recall:
Our photographs, like memories,
Have wilted, lost, or still stand tall
In wonder, by degrees. [5]

[1] This day was pink; the sky was clear.
[2] We made love on the couch, then floor.
[3] This trip we bought a souvenir.
[4] We always dreamed of something more.
[5] Love was our atmosphere.

Some Thoughts about You

There are many ways I think of you *being you*:
Sitting on the couch with reading glasses,
The back of you standing at the kitchen sink,
The stride of your gait where your shadow passes
Past me, and the way you make me wait.

I see you when you are not at home:
Your empty chair at the office desk,
Your decorous touches of earthy tones
Of reds and browns, your every task
Completed with such grace. Your vacant sounds.

I see you when you are not aware of being seen:
Working in the flowers, trimming a limb,
Washing windows on a ladder,
And me wondering if I could kiss you again
In the rain, or if this mattered.

Song of My (Younger) Self

The convict in his suit and tie has fled
Through fields subdued with juniper and flax,
The youthful bandit porting artifacts
Of bygone days, and memories, and shreds
Of decency. He stops to hail a cab,
Or holes up in some cheap, remote hotel
Awaiting word from his accomplice that
The coast is clear. He lives on bread and water
Writing ransom notes of thin disguise,
Creating plans to rob the bank, or bribe.
But after doing time, or posting bail,
The young con comes to plead his case, unwise
To all his past mistakes and paper trail
Too ironclad, and too fleeting, to deny.

The Sunday Afternoon

Home from church
      I sit down to write a sonnet
But I am interrupted by the sight of you
      Sleeping on the floor

And words I would have written
      Go unwritten where before
I would have finished
      What the day presented

But now I watch you sleeping
      Content in this afternoon
Hoping I will not disturb our peace
      Or you awake too soon

Breast Implants

The plastic surgeon seems to enjoy his work:
Holding the jelly orbs in his capable hands
And telling my wife that after her surgery
He will recreate what the cancer has taken.
How strange these are, jiggling in the light,
Resembling nothing I have cupped or kissed,
Hoping that after our world has been shaken
There is restoration in his expertise.

My wife selects her breast like a used car—
Testing the various models for their heft
And warming to the touch of one. We are
Happy with the choice and sign the line.
We trust there will be life in what is left,
And after silicone, more time.

Caribbean Cruise

The sea is blue. Our cabin spare. The service is extraordinaire.
The sky is aqua. Sunset red. The buffet is a myriad
Of escargot and caviar. We drink our wine late at the bar.

The sea is green.   The sunrise white. The taxi driver erudite.
The sky is turquoise. Island rust. The beach is ancient igneous.
The band is silver. Our faces tan. The ship is metropolitan.

The sea is purple. Sunset pink. We recline on the deck and think.
The evening black. The stars are white. We whisper and embrace the nigh
In love and laughter to discuss the colors miscellaneous.

The sea is ink. The hour late. Love holds us as we contemplate
The day now past.   The sky is blue. And I awaken next to you.

Not a Love Poem

Perhaps it is impossible to write without the "word"
Or the heart-bloom observations of the beloved
Despite what one knows about the calamitous world
And the burdens used to express it.

                              Nonetheless
A few may consider the rapturous yes
Captured in the underpinnings of the thought itself
Or I may watch you sleeping in uncovered silence
Fresh from your dress. *I could write this* . . .
                              but I digress.

10:00 p.m.

The sun has tucked behind Wyoming
On this Midwest night
A pale moon draped
Over the stiletto trees.
And somewhere on the continent
Two people are making love
In a quiet house
Draped in vinyl siding
While an old man snores
From his recliner
Across the street,
Or a mother is chasing
After the sound
Of little feet
Fresh from the soapy garden
Of their hiding.

Déjà Vu

One evening, while writing a book about breast cancer,
I suddenly had a tug of *déjà vu*,
The feeling that I had been writing this book for years
Inhabited by the ghosts of former lives.

But you were nowhere to be seen in the candlelight
As I was writing the book for you,
Writing, perhaps, to drive away the final night
Into the infinitesimal darkness of the new.

Equations We Have Known

$$(x + a)^n = \sum_{k=0}^{n} \binom{n}{k} x^k a^{n-k}$$

Light years from earth we strain to touch the stars
But never overcome the gravity
Of bodies bound by mass. Such entropy
Tugs back, defines us in the silent hours
When we have grown cold, or emptiness
Like vacuum's black, eats the oxygen
Of our energy and love's Newtonian
Formulas play out our days like chess.

I do, however, claim binomial
The evening's pull, the white moon's calculus,
The red wine poured and the firelight's crawl
Across the lacquered shadows of the wall
Where sparks ignite our tired souls, and blessed,
Collide in algebra, bodies at rest.

$$e^x = 1 + \frac{x}{1!} + \frac{x^2}{2!} + \frac{x^3}{3!} + \cdots, \qquad -\infty < x < \infty$$

All things expand:
Infinitesimal
In the cosmos' dark.

But in the matter
Of the human heart
All things converge.

And this world we create:
Domesticity's thrust
And the insatiable urge
Holds us together
For love's sake.

$$\sin\alpha \pm \sin\beta = 2\sin\frac{1}{2}(\alpha \pm \beta)\cos\frac{1}{2}(\alpha \mp \beta)$$

There was a time past when our days were free
When we were more than trigonometry
Or sines or cosines arcing toward some mass
Like angles pointing toward Pathagoras.
Back then we worked the problem, summarized
An answer more complex than first surmised.

Now we produce solutions as we should
Without desire to be misunderstood
Or flaunt such knowledge, as some might disgrace
The guilt of love upon the lover's face.
These lines we draw, familiar though mundane,
Slouch toward perfection of our Platonian plane.

$$A = \pi r^2$$

All things reside
Within the area
Of the circle's eye:
Love as we know it.
What we once were.
What we shall be.
And π.

The Gravity of Bodies

My love is not perfect
Merged to the entropy
Of my weaker man.

But if in imperfection
Love is pull enough
To gauge a plan,

Then I have theories
Why I could orbit you,
And can.

This is Not a Love Poem

This is not a love poem
Anymore than today is a song,
Nor are these thoughts expressed
Simply strung along
In randomness.

Rather, this is a testimony
To all the mundane
Sprinkled into our coffee mugs
And to the narrow lane
Where the postman, with a jerk,
Opens the gate
And shrugs
Beneath our greeting
Under the weight
Of his work.

LIFE

Twenty-one

A father begins his slow descent
The day his oldest daughter turns
Twenty-one. He wonders where she went.

And with each birthday subsequent,
As independence spikes and burns
A father begins his slow descent.

The best of youthful years were spent
In books and hopscotch taking turns.
At twenty-one, he wonders where she went.

A father mourns his age like Lent
And in repentance, as he yearns,
A father begins his slow descent.

He ponders if his life was meant
To teach the lessons that she learns
At twenty-one. He wonders where she went.

And in some future testament
Perhaps a daughter's love returns:
A father begins his slow descent
Past twenty-one.   And wonders where she went.

Sixteen

On my son's sixteenth birthday
I meet him after football practice
Among his avalanche of friends
To tell him I love him.
I tell him he is the joy of my life.

Tall and sweaty under his pads
He stares at me
As if I am a stranger
Who has just revealed to him
The most profound secret of the universe.

The Dorm

In the stifling heat of the college dorm
I help my daughter unload her books.
She is beautiful in her womanly form
Having inherited her mother's good looks.

We speak of nothing. The day wears on.
And I grow old in the tiny room
Recalling how soon and how far gone
Her life has flowered into bloom.

No longer needed, I turn to go,
Sweat-stained and sandal-clad.
My steps are heavy, measured, slow.
And she says, "Thank you, Dad."

The Graduate

Somewhere in these final months
Of games and weekend dances
We lost you to yourself and other
Bright alluring glances.

And now that you are you no more
But all together free
We hope that someday you'll return
To find eventually

That you had never really left
But quietly remain
Within the spaces you once knew
And where we spoke your name.

Home from Rugby Practice

My son says he played well
And does not need stitches
In the ear that is dangling
By a thread and beat to hell.

His grit of eighteen years
Has turned him into man
And left him bruised and
Unwilling to shed tears.

But I blanch and recoil
At the sight of his blood
And his open vein.

Impressed by his toil.
Proud in his pain.

Jesus Boy

He was a builder of clay birds
And wooden instruments of trade,
A godhead portioned into thirds
Still learning from the ones he made.

With every loaf he broke and blessed
A word resided in his hands
Which day-by-day his youth expressed
As honoring his own commands.

The Salutatorian

Here on the threshold of tomorrow
We greet life's possibilities with hope,
Eager to fulfill our horoscope
And embrace whatever paths our lives may follow.
We graduate into cliché,
Our aspirations high while deep in debt,
Feeling, somehow, that we shall not forget
Each sordid tryst or meaningless essay.

And should we find these years worthwhile,
Or lessons learned while in a state of grace,
Perhaps we shall redeem the time and smile
Through jobless prospects and the protocol
That turns the world and reveals face-to-face
The truths we do not know, but might learn, after all.

Natural Selection

On this spring morning I awake
And drape the sunlight across my shoulders
As I drift toward the coffee pot.

The air, it seems, is charged with energy
And I am eager to ignore the tasks
My wife has given me to accomplish.

Soon I will be sleeping in the hammock,
A newspaper for a blanket, and a birdsong
Rocking me in the sweet arms of sloth.

The Doppler Effect

The past, at varied distances,
Succumbs to thickness of the air
While sound and sound's forgetfulness
Stretches further in the mind,

Then pitches lower to deep sound
In the closest instances
Where memory rewinds,
And looking back,
Slips past the ears
Like a fast-train running
On a slick track,
Yet so indelibly defined.

Greek Grammar Lessons

εν Δοναλδ Ιεννερμαν, 1981

Ω, εισ, ει, ομεν, ετα, ουσι.
His active voice says, "Now you can parse
What Homer wrote, and dream his dream, and revel in his art."

Α, ασ, α, αμεν, ατε, αν.
He grasps our past tense with a yawn
And, like Homer, greets us with rosy fingers at the dawn.

The gods, Retired

The ancient ones, the gods of yore,
Now recline on their beds of stone,
No more concerned as was before
For plights of their humanities.
In bright Olympus, tired, alone,
They parse the works of Sophocles.

The dim stars of their progeny
Shine forth and mock the weaker tears
Of daughters and the sons of men
Who, as Lucretius spurned their hand,
Recoil in horror at their ease
And weep no longer for their prayers.

Autumn Kaleidoscope

What colors cleave
May morph and may
Yet bloom and bloom
To blue of day

Or run as red
Hues as hues arc
Green into crimson
And beautiful dark

The Son in the Basement

At the midnight hour I startle,
Awakened by the crash of barbell
On the basement floor.

I lie in bed upstairs,
Bewildered by your anguished pain
Beyond the bedroom door.

And suddenly the night is filled
With an excruciating love
That will not give me rest.

I lie there in the darkness
Listening as you lift me
Light as air. And I am blessed.

Odysseus Meets Tiresias in Hades

O kind Tiresias, return once more and prophesy
Of this final journey into death,
This earthly realm of Hades, void of breath,
From which none may return to testify.

O kind Tiresias, speak comfort to my soul,
For I must cross the River Styx
With coin in hand, as death predicts,
And enter into shadow by this toll.

And you, Tiresias, kind friend and honest guide,
Do not begrudge this last request
Returning to my loves, as I've confessed:
But let my name be blessed and dignified.

Centuries

Had we lived in some distant century
Our path, our world, would have been dimmed by night
With half the day unfit for work or sight
And each decision lorded by decree.

Our work would be the candle and the flame,
The full week's labors lifted up by song
In search of food and water, and the long
Return back home to where kin knew our name.

The only true insurance was the spear
And any scratch or madness led to death.
The span of life was like an evening's breath
And creature comforts were the hearth and beer.

So few there were who lived to dark and gray
When all was superstition and decay.

Butcher, Baker

How simple life was, once primeval,
When names reflected occupation
And guilds were keys to wealth and station
In the world of the Medieval.

The Butcher hacked, the Baker baked,
The Carpenter was hammer, nail.
The Sailor would unfurl his sail
And thirst for glory never slaked.

The Tinker formed his silver dam,
The Painter was his brush and tint,
The Priest was prayer and firmament,
The Shepherd crook, and goat and ram.

Each name reflected path and plan,
The tools and talent of a trade.
The world was thereby shaped and made
By no dream larger than the hand.

Consider the Birds
—Matthew 6:26

Consider the birds of the air:
Their arc, their race,
The moving firmament
Suspended on the face
Of the sun's stare
At their swift descent.

These have not fallen in
Error from God's grace
As we have from our birth,
But in joy embrace
Our tired and sullen sin,
And wing us back to earth.

Red Shift

Light years from earth, a boomerang
Of radiation—violets, blues—
Glows within the rim of the Big Bang.
The giant stars, like Betelgeuse,

Emit a trail of gamma rays
That shift in space and time at speed
Of light. The Doppler Effect gravitates
The purple-violet haze and bleeds

The energy to red. Quasars
Are mysteries, as are Black Holes.
Yet in the memory of stars
We glimpse creation of our souls:

Vast eons through the telescope
Where light bleeds dying into hope.

An Easter Prayer

We are no longer impressed
By the birth of green
Or the spring of photosynthesis
Nor have we seen
Miracle in the seed's helix creed
Or the holy scripture
Of the maple leaf.

We pray the air
Hoping we may be raised
Through the world's grief
By some distant God
Who has come near
Through the stone
Heart of our belief.

Milkweed

There is a blessing in this long row of milkweed
The parachutes of seed transporting me back
To a boy walking along a country road
His gaze fastened to a dancing dragonfly
And a mother far beyond earshot
Calling him home for dinner.

Advent

The leaves have at last slipped from the trees
And capped the snail trails along the concrete steps,
With winter tasks completed, windows caulked
Beside the smooth inebriations of chimney smoke.

We feel a portent wafting on cold breeze:
An omen marked by frost upon the panes.
The wind snatches the notes that we once spoke,
And in the silence children huddle like refrains.

The fires are stoked, the quilts folded with ease
Around the margins like an envelope,
And every hearth that opens its mouth to sing
Emits a fear not greater than its hope.

An Advent Prayer

These dark days
Kaleidoscope
Into arrays
Of texture
Which we grope
For as we drive
Across town.
We feel so alive—
Though we drown
Inside ourselves
Seduced by bows
And those bright toys
We cannot buy.
But when hope fails,
The lights premier
And gladden our hearts
With a love
We cannot name,
And do no fear.

The Christ Child's Prayer

For years I said *I love you*
Late on these Christmas Eves,
Wrought in the wonder of the new
And the world's old griefs.

But hearts are neither lighter
Nor wounds and scars less deep
Now that the world is brighter
With belief.

And so I give you these
Small gifts of gospel word
Hoping they may serve to ease
As eager heard,

Some ancient sin now pardoned,
Or stranger taken in—
That you may know eternal joy . . .
And my life without end.

Superman

When the phone rings I don my special suit and tie
And drive across town to the railroad tracks where a man has died.
The fire chief and police greet me there and ask that I
Escort the company of family to a room nearby.

They are stacked there—tear on tear and friend on friend—
Anticipating that my super powers will bring a swift end
To the injuries they bleed and that I will soon defend
The innocent and offer explanation for what they cannot comprehend.

But I have no answers and my weakness is my might.
My speed is touch without x-ray sight.
My cape is tattered, and when they ask me to explain their plight,
My words are mine—*and these are kryptonite.*

Redbuds

They pop onto the proboscis of spring
      Like chicken pox
Randomly infecting everything
      Borne of air
We breathe them deeply
      For few days
Until their pink infection strays
      To other phlox
And suddenly they disappear

Maundy Thursday

A friend once asked me to explain
What it felt like to stand behind
The altar and speak
The words: "This is my body,
This is my blood" while breaking bread
And lifting cup.

And I admitted that it was much
Like inviting guests to a dinner
I had not prepared,
And that, though embarrassed,
I assumed the Host would soon arrive
And would be startled to find *me* there.

Communion

This is the feast of perfect faith:
An apple and a golden pear
Quartered on the plate,
The Lord of heaven incarnate
And tabernacled here.

Rooms

For Vicki

When we were young there were rooms
Lined with belching radiators
Coat racks, blackboards, a phonics chart,
And desks in perfect rows.

And in each, there was a teacher who would teach:
Science perhaps, or health, or art,
Knowing what it was that children know
Or how far they could reach.

The rooms were a habitation
Of families known by name
Alphabetized for simplicity,
Gold stars licked in a frame.

In each room there were secret histories
That only the teacher knew
And what their futures held, and who was who,
And teaching was a conversation.

Some rooms smoldered in September heat
Or frosted in the January glare
While every student, incomplete,
Would build a home room there.

Each room revealed distinctive paths,
Unique or broad, as each learned
A body of knowledge, practical crafts,
Or how to multiply and add.

Through time the teacher understood
What these rooms held for each,
Or for generations if her perseverance could
Make that farthest leap

Into those rooms leading to other rooms
Where the secret histories now reach
Into other lives, into other minds,
Through the teacher who would teach.

My Mother's Arms

Then they were young and lithe and strong
When my body was her baby
And the full length of me a song
Singing her only child.

Then as they firmed in adolescent's strife
They coaxed, and taught, and barred the door.
In short, they birthed me into life
And gave to me the world, and more.

Then they were tired and tiring
And deserving of rest,
Having completed those tasks
Which once had blessed.

And at the last mottled with age,
Yet supple and supine,
When they have become too weak to bear her home—
I shall give her mine.

My Father's Legs

My father once walked upon the earth
And when he ran there was wind in his hair
And my short steps could not keep up.

Then years he labored standing on his feet
And loomed as hero over me:
A boy, who watched him work in the day's heat.

In time there came a moment when
My strength was more than his
And I could beat him to the basket with a spin.

Then, as a son mourns his father's age,
I fell again behind his footsteps
And helped him struggle with a cane.

And since my father's legs have died
I see his love and the light in his face.
At rest. But still running in place.

Ideas

First there was fire, then words,
Then charcoal smeared on walls.
But *a priori* these were merely thoughts
Like butterflies that no one could catch
And no way to name them.
These have been dancing on the winds
Of time since the beginning
And have come here from the ancestors
Who are still releasing them
Like pollen, into the atmosphere.

In Praise of Women

Men see them everywhere:
At work; the gym; the laundromat;
Awakened by the surprise
Of their varied smiles
And their acrobatic eyes;
These life-givers, who incite
To such excitement
The strut or show of strength
Or the great lengths
Men go to gain attention
Or to sit in obeisance
To the scent of estrogen;
How these arouse from dream
The aspirations and energies
Of testosterone
As in the distance gleam
The brighter lights of love
And mountains
And imponderable seas.

Drums

Some are beating quick in warm blood
Or fired in the furnace of need
While other rhythms like majors beat
Involuntary through their years

And others leap in frantic pace
As pistons lubed in ventricles
Or the heightened sensations
Fueled by burning sex

But in eventuality each stills
To silence like a song past sung
And the last beat echoes
With a peaceful resonance

Geometry

A few are squares
Living in dark holes
Or pegs that do not fit,
While some, rectangular,
Portion days like blocks
Of calendar
Wholly separate.
And others are triangular
In approach or benefit,
Neither saint, nor sage,
Nor hypocrite,
But loops and parallels
And lines that defy
A measurement.

The world is round.
And that's the shape of *it*.

Sunday Morning

What legion of angels has marched
Through this morning's morning light
And sacrificed their haloes to the dawn?

Autumn

We are drunk on the scent of yellow:
The maples reaching for the arching blues
Of cloudless sky,
The wrens and finches
Propping up the feeders and the benches
Streaked with stains of fresh chartreuse.
The grass is bent and measured by
The welcome shadow of the bus
Where children fly from yellow doors
Enjoined in serendipitous
Shrieks of laughter.
And raking lawns we mark the time
By foliage fallen from the trees,
Their veins and codices sublime
To make us float upon their seas
Of roiling wind-swept atmosphere
Where, drenched in color, we appear.

Questions in the Night

We do not fear
The cancer diagnosis,
The crash, the burn,
The long prognosis.
Nor do we fear
The fear itself
Or the heart's hollows,
But the silences
Where we must live
In all that follows.

Chemotherapy

You are still you inside the golden skin.
I see you behind your kind and steady eyes
Where you have opened your welcoming
Smile to let yourself in.

You are still you as your cheeks are fair.
I see you inside yourself where surprise
Surfaces for a laugh
And you find yourself there.

Houdini Speaks to His Widow

Someday, when all my tricks have fled,
I shall slip out among the stars, though dead,
And drift among the silver points of light.

I shall reach out, though shackled by
My lack of form—to say goodbye.
(Though slight-of-hand is best performed by night.)

And no straightjacket, ankle cuff,
Or water torture strong enough
Will bind me here, released from nature's laws.

Forget me not, but speak my name,
A one-night-only candle flame.
But for my final act hold your applause.

On My Daughter's Wedding Day

How lovely your years have collided on this day
Of laughter, love, and indelible light,
Your face a flower, your dress a bouquet
Of memories in white.

Your smile and beauty makes your father blessed,
Though as I grieve your years exhaled
I wish I could through love's excess
Redeem where I have failed.

I see you slip away, coiled in his arms,
My child, my fair phenomenon,
Desiring to save you both from this world's harms
And kiss you with a song.

A Prayer on My Daughter's Wedding Day

Would it be selfish, Lord, to pray for gifts
Of such illimitable, marvelous wonder—
Poured from your gracious hand, unsung or
Unrelenting—as my provision drifts

In a father's weakness, though my love
Is strong? And could I ask for such as these:
But a bountiful earth, the salt of seas,
And guiding stars arrayed in splendor above?

May these two know such joys and sweetened leaven
In all their days ahead, such as you give.
And may their years bless us, as you forgive,
To carry them, at last, across the threshold of your heaven.

On the First Anniversary of His Wife's Death

He thinks that time will heal. But this is fable.
He tries to call her friends. But is not stable.
He wants to venture out. But is not able.
Her photograph remains upon the table.

Jerald

We found him slumped in the garbaged alley
Behind the church,
Stiff-white knuckles forcing the bottle
To his thin lips.
We carried him away
Angelically
In winter winds
To a decent burial beyond the county road.
Resurrected from the mounded grave we proceeded
Hastily to our pews . . .
Soiled with duty and with yesterday's news.

Alternative Christmases

Every December 24th
I sit in church on Christmas Eve—
Filled of fruitcake, carols and mirth,
Seized by the Spirit and belief
That God finds faith upon the earth.

But I confess, in pondering mind,
How soon my interests—warmed and piqued—
Mull questions of a richer kind:
Wondering what others—alone, fatigued—
Find holy in their daily grind?

I imagine a woman in Abilene
Reading a greasy paperback,
Thumbing through her magazine,
Slick advertisements and her lack
A gospel obtuse and obscene.

I see a man inside a bar
Asking the waitress for octane,
His stool and coaster escritoire
Recording drams of the mundane
Contours of women and cigar.

And I, formed in the liturgy
Of candlelight and holly-wreath,
Freely admit that I could be
Content with these spared of belief,
And worship in their jubilee.

Nativity Somnambulism

The habitation of sugar plums
Is the child's excited dream
Wrapped in the crèche's gospel scheme
And fed on hopes and sucking thumbs.

Induced by scents of cookie night
She wakes and rises before dawn
And greets the morning with a yawn
Like Jesus entering the light.

World Without End

Before the lust for trade and commerce
The redwood punctured the lonely stars
As there were no worlds in the universe
To consider ours.

The wolf and bear, ancestral foes,
Were worshipped in the night primeval,
Before God donned His divine clothes
In the cathedral.

The Angel Speaks Glad Tidings to the Shepherds

The foreigner has not retreated from the land,
Nor have the poor been fed on the promises
Of the powerful as they calmly discuss
The means of war and how it can expand.

But yet the world is loved. Who can condemn?
For the wide road leads to Herod's bloody hand,
And the narrow path to Bethlehem.

Christmas Lights

Every perfect gift is from above,
coming down from the Father of Lights
—James 1:17

In these dark days past equinox
The old ways order the songs we sing,
The earth grown cold in paradox
While stars announce a reckoning
Inherent in each living thing.

With hope celestial, born below,
We ponder lights and ascertain
A grace-filled spirit from their glow,
Anticipating their domain
May transform what we cannot know.

The Goddess of Little Things

—for Ruth Neeley

She was the goddess of little things:
Buttons, thread, thimbles, strings,
Knick-knacks, books, baskets, mats,
Knobs, photo albums, hats.
She was the picture of penmanship
With stationery, postcards, a quip
Of wisdom gently offered up
In frying pans and coffee cup.
Each closet, drawer and place entailed
A life lived out—full and detailed.

Watering the Roses on a Saturday Morning

The sun's orange eye is staring
At these red blooms with envy,
As I, the intermediary,
Nozzle a spray while sharing
A familiar nod with the mailman's truck.

The blooms, so effervescent with
A sugar plum of cinnamon, bequeath
Their beauty, pluck by pluck,
As my last will and testament
Is eulogized. And I, as dead
Inside the bloom these blooms have built beneath
This brilliant sky,
Am laid to rest in summer's luck,
Sealed in a wreath of red.

Inside This Day

There is another day
That you will remember
For what did not occur
Within the boredom
Of routines or the exacting
Rituals of the rehearsed.
But you will be blessed
To recall in gratitude
Some small act
Or kindness
That was not there at first.
And in remembering
The day versed
In memory of what
It could have been
But was not,
You would have
Lived it well
Long before
You had not
Lived it
Or forgot.

Three Versions of Myself

I live three versions of myself:
A halo some project on me,
An archetype as on a shelf
Admired through mediocrity.

My twin is father to the whole
And lover to my wife's caress,
Though few confuse me with the soul
Who loves sex' metamorphosis.

I triplicate into the real,
A blueprint with no diagram:
I tell myself what I should feel
And live my version as I am.

Good Friday, New York

Standing in the shadow of Atlas
I count the people entering St. Patrick's Cathedral
Who make the sign of the cross.

Five enter, somber and downcast,
While eight, gripped in awe,
Flash fingers curled, and at the last
Step, pause . . . as if holding up the world.

Three Ekphrastic Sonnets Written
After Visiting the Chicago Gallery of Art

I.

American Gothic, by Grant Wood

This could be any farm, or any two,
And that's the beauty of it, I suppose.
The notion that Grant Wood might misconstrue
And paint a house between a thorn and rose.
The sky is blue, we see that clear enough,
But something dour and juxtaposed is there
Upon the canvas, and the faces rough
With weather. Their smiles are little more than threadbare
Hints of happiness, and their eyes
Averted slightly toward the scene's context:
A presence which the form itself implies
Is absence. Yet the subjects know that next
To them is still-life, with pitchfork in hand.
A family farm upon a vanished land.

II.

Portrait of Elizabeth I by Nicholas Hilliard, 1585

The lighted window, glazed with leaded glass,
Secludes the realm of wealth and circumstance
In palace walls devoid of any glance
Or faint attachment to the broad expanse
Of lands and commerce where her subjects pass.

A golden sword rests on the blackened throne,
An ermine, white and eager, climbs her sleeve
As if Her Highness, removed and naïve,
Could stir a grateful nation to believe
That she was worthy of the world they own.

The portrait, cold and austerely serene,
Reveals the common love of pedigree
When every knee bows to pomposity
And worships rags if they be called a Queen.

III.

Nighthawks, by Edward Hopper

What is it Hopper hoped to paint in black?
A scene? A feeling? A simple time and place?
Or are these strokes of genius the hidden face
Of the artist himself? Would an insomniac
Recognize this café as his own, or drink
A cup of coffee at the bar? Would lonely
Hearts seek vacant streets like this, or only
Make their way to this illumined ink
Of canvas?
           We peer inside ourselves, our soul
Observing dour slats of light—a slow,
Methodical form of rituals, a quilt
Of sadness shadowed by the night, the glow
Of past lives moving through us, our guilt
Congregating in the only church we know.

Horizon

I could see you coming for a long time
    As from a great distance
        Where earth and sky meet:
A miniature form,
    Little more than a stick
        Without head, arms, feet.
It was years before
    I knew all of you
        Or could see you replete
With detail approaching
    Over that vast plain
        As if rising from heat.
But isn't this true?
    To behold love at a distance
        We behold it incomplete?

Time Was

Time was when I saw time
As all the time in the world
   As time to ignore such hours
   As hours slip golden by
   And a dark hush swoons
   Across the sky.

Time now as time defines
The broken circle breaks
   As time in distant history
   As hours fleeting hurled
   And yearning for time's love
   In the weak arms of the world.

When We Were Gods

When we were gods
       The earth was a garden of delights
       For our enjoyment, and the fruit
       Was for the taking—so we ate.
       Though neither rugged nor astute
       We prowled, and fancied that the nights
       Were ours to love and liberate.

       We conquered lands and quaffed the dregs
       Of every fresh exciting sex
       Condemned by Titans or taboo.
       The world was not yet dark, complex,
       Or pained by injuries or aches,
       And each decision impromptu.

When we were gods
       We took no thought of mortal quest
       Across the sea in search for truth,
       Or dreamed as did Odysseus
       Of wisdom rather than our youth.
       There were no sins to be confessed,
       And though not blessing we were blessed.

       Such beauty as the world defines
       Was disregarded in our haste,
       To lift ourselves as primary
       Chalice of the wine's great grace.
       We patterned life by our designs
       Without an intermediary.

When we were gods
     The mountains were just epoch's hills.
     The forests had not yet sprung forth
     To wrap their rooted, lazy clutch
     Around our souls. There was no north.
     We ravaged time. We swallowed pills.
     The sun was still cold to our touch.

     We were immortal in those days
     When, stretched before us, like a pall,
     We laughed at death, we harrowed hell,
     And winged our flight before our crawl.
     There was a chorus sang our praise
     Before we stooped toward earth, and fell.

The Death of the Greek Professor
—for Donald Jennerman

Within the architecture of
Gothic spire and Roman arch
He ranked in learning far above
His students in their eager search
And kindly offered them the torch

Of Homer and his Odyssey.
In time they mastered dialect,
Euclidian geometry,
And opined in the intellect
Of each philosophy and sect.

They read of gentle Socrates
And of Platonic metaphors,
As well as in Thucydides'
And Anaxagoras' storied lores
Of the Peloponnesian wars.

And he, professor by degrees,
Was αλφα and ωμεγα man—
Who smiled with Aristophanes,
And dreamed of Plato's perfect land
Above the darker Styxian.

He sleeps now in the shadowed earth
Of netherworld and Sappho's verse
Awaiting neither death nor birth,
Nor Oracle of hope adverse
To any blessing or the curse.

But if, perchance, as Socrates
Concluded just before his draught—
He goes to meet Diogenes,
To seek in honest truth his craft
Of teaching students while he laughed.

The Scarecrow

For weeks I watched his wicked stare entice
My better angel from the avenue
Below the railroad tracks. His merchandise

Heaped in a shopping cart of residue,
The tattered remnants of his straw-man mind.
I greeted him, he flashed his blue tattoo,

And presently our souls became entwined.
I fed him coats and scarves and pocket change
While he recoiled in cold at humankind.

Our conversation was an odd exchange
Of metaphors and meager sustenance,
Though neither found the other wholly strange

To make us question how our quick romance
Could leave us, unchanged, in our circumstance.

The World Premier

Each day I rise before the sun
To meditate upon my coffee grounds,
To mark the silence inside these lonely sounds
And ponder new beginnings before they have begun.
The welcome of the whippoorwill
Is like a ticket-taker in the cold
Where possibilities redeem the old
And morning lights with wings upon the window sill.
A train blows in the distant dark—
A speck of history written in review
Closes the door upon the night's curfew
And points to the horizon toward which I shall embark.
The dawn, premiering in this matinee,
Opens the curtain on another day.

Hummingbirds

Momentary guests, these spirits breeze
Along the rows of foxglove on bright wing,
Light from light, swift color carrying
Their gospel from each petal to the trees.
And on each pause, while beak imbibed in flowers,
We strain to note the outline of their eyes.
Such tiny ghosts, their busyness belies
A graceful dance which we could watch for hours.
In quick succession, colors come and go:
The darting green, chartreuse, the airy blues,
Crimson, lavender, and varied hues
That race our hearts to stir, though we don't know
Where these originate, nor how, nocturn,
If in their departing, shall return.

The Greek Professor Offers His Apology

And now we forward to page fifty-nine
Where in his mortal quest Odysseus
Descends to Hades. Here, Tiresius,
The blind and aged seer offers sign,
And warns our hero not to venture forth.
But what are we to learn when life dissuades
Our hopeful progress? What cold and scornful shades
Do we encounter as we gauge the worth
Of our life's efforts? And what are the shields
We carry with us? Friends, these quests converge
In timeless journeys as the demiurge
Created us to seek Elysian Fields.
But first the Styx awaits, then welcome shade.
This river is wide. And the toll must be paid.

Vacancy
—for L.

Had you survived the overdose
You would be thirty-one today
And we would be sitting in a restaurant
Talking about my grandchild
Or how your day had gone
With all of its undulations
Of work and play
Or laughing over dessert
About your father and our sex
Or how lovely the day has been
While hugging in the parking lot
And making plans for the next
Time we'd meet for lunch
But this is your birthday
And I have eaten alone
Marking another year
With a big black X
And wondering how one expects
To make it through such days
When the sun is shining
And the world is awake
With promise and delight
But inside it is raining
And I am still expecting you
To blow out the candles on your cake.

The Father Considers His Depressed Son

For months now I have longed to crawl
    Into the dark hole of your mind
To peer into the closets closed
    Wondering what I'd find

There in that state of consciousness
    Where you have lost your will to care
And conversations once enjoyed
    Have wilted in despair

In spite of my best promises
    And all the vile and thorny prayer
Still vigilant I'll hold the light
    And hope to meet you there

Lullaby

You soothe our bad and violent dreams
  Of such horrendous, callous deaths
  And counterparts of sleeping in short-shallow breaths
Where imagination stirs much darker than life seems.

And if, perchance, we do not wake
  But set sail in a sea of tranquil blue,
  By morning may we rouse, refreshed and new
To hum your melody, though our hearts should break.

Blessing

I remember the day my father died.
This was also the day I was born.
We were standing in a field
Freshly turned and planted,
A field that had worn our hands
Rough with clods, the scent
Of damp earth under our feet.
And my father did not shelter me
From the scorching heat,
He did not condescend
Or offer me rest from the labor.
Plodding through mud, he said,
"This is the way it is. This will be your life."
That afternoon, my father gave
His life for me out of his own
Hardship and weariness.
And when he placed his hand on my head
And tousled my hair,
I received his blessing and felt
His hope transcend to me.
And I was born.

The crows were witnesses.

The Pileated Woodpecker

The Spotting

This past spring—on a cool morning with coffee cup in hand—I
spied the pileated woodpecker through the dawn mist. Clinging to
the trunk of the hackberry tree, the bird was magnificent—long,
lean, and crested with a flaming-red plume that exploded against
the earth-tone gray of the hackberry bark. Motionless, the bird
remained in its vertical hold for long minutes, a kind of snapshot, a
brush-stroke of color amid the ripe green leaves of spring.
Suddenly, the bird released and, instead of falling, rose majestically
through a canopy of maple, buckeye and oak until it disappeared
against the backdrop of morning sky.

The Deck Feeder

Another morning, days later, I am reunited with the woodpecker as
it perches on a rotting squirrel -feeder that the previous home
owners had nailed to the trunk of the hackberry. This is an odd
picture, as I have never seen a pileated searching for food in a
feeder. But the bird pauses, as if studying the situation, and then
offers a few faint-hearted taps upon the rotted wood. There are no
grubs in the pores of the feeder and the bird's attention is suddenly
wrested away by a harsh gush of wind that stirs the leaves. As the
bird wings away, I stand at the window and wonder: *where does
the woodpecker find comfort, and where does it go for solace from
the storm?*

The Siding

It is mid June. Striding along the path near the creek I hear the echo
of a *rap-rap-rap* on the side of the house. I locate a clear vista and
peer up onto the eastern face of our home. There, clinging to the
house, is the pileated woodpecker drilling its bill into my wood
siding. Even from my distance, I can see that the bird has culled a

silver-dollar-sized hole in the dry rot. I flinch at the thought, but am then suddenly moved by the awe of the hunt. The giant crest of the pileated bobs and shudders as it feeds on the miniscule. The waters of the creek slip silently along behind me and, for a moment, my attention is focused on a small yellow dot of flower that is peeking through the dirt along the hardened path where I am walking. When I look up again, the woodpecker is gone.

The Silence

I consider the woodpecker one afternoon in early July while I am mowing the yard. Days have passed without a sighting. *Would anyone dare to assume a woodpecker's joy?*

The Return

Mid July, I am reunited with the pileated woodpecker. It clings, as before, to the bark of the hackberry on a summer morning. As the bird angles its head away from me, I can see that its beak is disproportionally long—a kind of curved straw. The beak is the lifeblood of the pileated. The beak is its hope. With wings flattened against its slender body, suddenly the woodpecker opens like a trap door and, after a moment's descent, rises like a breath on the summer air and is gone.

The Last Sighting

As I amble up the lawn, firewood in hand, suddenly the woodpecker appears in a clearing—a kind of spark, a flame flush against the verdant background of the trees. Red against green, I cannot miss the bird as it steps, talon-prone, inch by inch up the side of a towering sycamore. Weak-armed, I stoop to deposit the firewood on the lawn and gaze up into the summer sky to study the bird again. It is toying with me. Showing off as children do. Or so it seems. The pileated shakes its plume at me—a wisp of blood-red feathers, fine as powder, and I can see the ends dancing in the early

August heat. The woodpecker pauses. We stare at each other. Our meeting ends when the bird issues a guttural cry and sails across the creek into a deep morass of maple and walnut.

The Death

Carrying the morning newspaper under my arm, I discover the pileated woodpecker on the gravel driveway beneath the large bow window of my home office. It is dead. Perhaps in early morning or the night before, it had flown-into the reflection of the window and broken its neck. I kneel, set aside the newspaper, and cusp the bird in my hands. It is still warm. I marvel at the size of the bird, perhaps eighteen inches in length, and as the morning light crosshatches the trees I note that the bird's feathers are a myriad of color, a rainbow embedded in the darker navy-black of the body, and the distinguishing red plume ripe with hints of white and yellow. The eyes are closed, and the rims dotted with curious dots of raised skin. The talons are coal black, sharp as needles. I wrap the bird in a section of newspaper classifieds and wonder how a woodpecker experiences its own color, its own existence? I carry the bird down to the creek accompanied by the dirge of songbirds and the rustling of mid-August leaves announcing the end of summer. I remove my shoes and wade into the creek. The water is effervescent. I bend over and hold out the section of newspaper containing the pileated woodpecker.

The Release

The hardest part is the letting go.

Today I Shall Sit in Silence

Today I shall sit in silence,
Disregarding the news
Of greed and death,
And find my solace in
The music of the whippoorwill.

I shall regard the breath
Of the summer breeze
And listen to the trill
Of cicada song
In the sycamore trees.

I shall be still
And unaware of all
I deem my own,
Until the moon peeks
Over the horizon
Where the sun has set,
And the day has blown.

Window to the Soul

I used to be that man, who home from distant cities,
Would stand for hours at the window looking out
Upon the dissolution of the seasons,
Inspired by labor's loves and blind committees.
But as for distance, there were reasons.
And youthful certitudes trumped every doubt.

Now here I am, past prime and worn through,
A man who stares at his reflection long
After the shaving cream has dripped and dried,
A faint shadow of his former self, construed
Of pasted pieces of a life, and a weak song
That steals on open ears, though magnified.

I have resigned myself to questioning
The tuft of grass, the clouds, the buckeye leaves,
And the morning's silence that will not speak
In hurried cadences, or demands anything
Other than to be still in the world's mystique
And search for joy, though all about me grieves.

I am that man, who hurried home from war,
Has lost large portions of his soul to things
That long have forfeited their lust-allure,
And at the window of his last years, gazing in,
Has returned to his love, and reckonings
Of all he had forgotten, to begin again.

LIGHT

One Percent

For years he studied business books
And read the *Wall Street Journal*
Certain that he had the looks
And could live his life nocturnal.

He made a fortune, spent it twice,
And built it yet again
Through marriages and varied vice
And market discipline.

And then one day he realized
His life had come and went,
With nothing sure or certified
Except his one percent.

Skin

Some wear it thin
And others thick.
Pigs give it when
The kickers kick.

Some are taken in
Or fleeced and then
Flayed like men
Who sin.

But there is deep
And tanned ten
And shorn sheep
In dad's den.

And now and then
We win by teeth
Or fall asleep
In what lies beneath.

Old Golfers

They swing is spasms of half-arc
Through firm, arthritic hips,
Peripheral, wide of the mark,
And par by nine iron chips.

Their bags are light as scrotums hang
Through slacks of sansabelt,
And half their drives—a boomerang—
Return to leave a welt.

Deliberate, they pad the grass
Through careful steps of tweed,
Putting on greens rolled smooth as glass
Through breaks they cannot read.

But each is paring out for pride
Though double-bogies reign,
And every Titleist hooked wide
Induces sudden pain.

But at the clubhouse, rolling in,
They settle up their bets,
Each sucking at their oxygen
And scoring no regrets.

The Death of the Wall Street Trader

Initially his life defined
By milk and Oreos
Grew increasingly refined
By girls and stereos.

He grew and inch, he ran a mile,
Perpetual in motion,
And with each competing smile
Was offered a promotion.

His house was rave, his pool immense,
His family perfection,
His stocks and bonds grew by percents
And hedged him in protection.

But when the market crashed and burned
In 1929
He spurned the lessons he had learned
And mocked the warning sign.

Some say his loss was his demise
But others so allege
His fortune merely magnified
The distance from his ledge.

Punctuation

Comma

Consider the breath stalled
In the chimney of the throat
Or picture the painter
Removing the brush from the canvas
Ever so slightly—
The rhythm of bristles
Rising and falling
Like a sigh.
And when the writer writes
Attempting to create words
That sing . . .
These breaths and brush strokes
Cling to the hinge
Of such a small
Small thing.

Semi-colon

A door opens and closes
As do the gates
Of ancient cities
And the synapses
Of the mind.

And on the page
There is a joint
Where one thought closes
And another opens
And both come together
To make the one
Most beautiful point.

Parentheses

((Considerations aside)
Interior monologue
Is often captured
In nets
And even
The unspoken
Ponderings
One remembers
Or forgets.
And between
These bookends
One discovers
A refugee
Lost in the far country
Of a familiar home.)

(Parenthetically)

Ampersand

Red and White is connected to Blue
As are lawyers to their firms
As well as stand-up comedy teams.

Fish with Chips seems
As natural in polarity
As sky drawn to sand
Or words on a page.

Foam with sea
Rubber with band
& so forth, etc. &

Colon

Some thoughts cannot be canned
But must be given air
So they can breath
If only through two holes
Punched and planned
In a creativity
As locked in prison
And then set free.

Question Mark

How can I influence your thought
But by asking what you think?
And why would you let me in
Unless I knock?

Period

All good things must come to an end:
The star-studded movie at the multiplex,
The bull market, the vacation,
The amazing sex.

The writer must grant permission
To part with a thought
So that another can begin
As it most certainy ought.

Closet

Hanging on the closet rack
Are khakis, linens, corduroys,
Blue jeans, sweats, and in the back
A pair of long johns. A turquoise

Button-down for golf is clipped
Inside a blazer. And alone—
Inside the plastic as it shipped—
An overcoat of herringbone.

The rainbow hues of summer wear
Are stashed on hooks, a few Hawaiian;
And ties displayed—so debonair—
Through strips of metal with the eye in

Each a Windsor Knot. Beneath
The clothing, on the carpet, shoes
On tightened wooden trees bequeath
A nose of leather and diffuse

Their oddly-aromatic traces.
The vacant hangers shift, extrude,
And beckon me to take their places
As I slip out of the nude.

The Snowman in Summer

He dreams deep, dying of leaf to frost,
The windshields covered with hominy dew,
When the sun consumes in its holocaust
The remains of an old year not yet new.

With coal-black eyes, though apropos,
He twists his stick arms avant-garde,
Entombed in sleep until the snow
Shall resurrect him in the yard.

Midas Touch

His office walls, littered with plaques,
Reveal the honors of his purse,
Their varies seals and signatures
A light among his artifacts.
His desk shines of mahogany,
His leather chair a lustrous hue
Announcing his plush revenue
Which he obtained through pedigree.
And yet for all his wealth and more
He guards in Swiss banks to retain,
He dreams large how he might obtain
A headline deal for his encore.
He lives each day complete, controlled,
Untouched, impoverished in gold.

To Old Men

They no longer flinch at the clap of thunder
Nor rise to work at first light,
But have succumbed to their boyhood wonder
And visions in the night.

They are tired enough to glimpse
Life's beauty in slow-motion:
Sails, and warm sunlight as it limps
Across the distances of ocean.

They are not frightened by silent rooms
Nor the absences of friends,
As they have shed their young costumes
And have made amends.

They are quiet when they speak
But their words hold weight
Because they know the world's mystique
And the faults that educate.

They do not change when death is near
Nor note with painful sigh
What the world tells them they must hear
Nor falsely glorify.

They do not age past certain points
But hold themselves together
By fortitude and arthritic joints
Which swell in stormy weather.

They do not need to speak, but in
The silence they are strong,
Nor confuse words for discipline,
Nor self-allure as song.

They grind to a halt like rusty cogs
And silent take their leave
Trailing behind rich monologues
With no tricks up their sleeve.

Fraternity Song

They touted Ovid, said that sex
Would save me from the intellects,
And told me Romanesque romance
Would get me in her underpants.

But then I learned that Aristotle
Lived alone and hit the bottle,
Alexander battled gay,
And Sophocles—he liked ballet.

So as I learned to parse the verb
I earned degrees and lost my nerve,
No longer casting Homer's pearls
Believing they would win me girls.

You

Some guys score on the business trip and others scope the beach,
While I've watched women from afar bloom slowly out of reach.
Powerful men have mistresses, and young men have affairs,
While I sit here with you each night and softly say my prayers.

And some I know have girls in tow and later notch their belt,
While others yet try to forget just what it was they felt
When love was plush and they felt the rush of hormones spurting new.
But when was I ever that crafty or clever at finding another but you?

The Old Married Couple Reflects on Why
They Didn't Need eHarmony.com

Ours was *not* love at first sight
Or born of some insatiable lust . . .
This came later, in hindsight,
And was the plan that we discussed.

Ours was not filtered through the lens
Of jealousy or deep respect,
Nor any online disciplines
Of mutual goals or intellect.

Ours was no love that, prearranged,
Decided probability,
Nor individually estranged
Toward deep compatibility.

Ours was the work of sacrifice
Assuming no love is a given,
And *then* we touched the merchandise
And kissed our little piece of heaven.

The Luddite

My tools of trade are parchment, pen.
The car I drive is old and gray.
I doubt the world of digital
And find no value in this day
Of quick and easy throw-away.

The toil I give is bone and sweat.
The world I knew is in the past.
TV has dimmed my gaze, and yet
I only see what's moving fast,
Though haste is never built to last.

I work in words upon the page
And love to feel the human touch.
But I am living in the age
When news is just celebrity
And having debt is deemed as much.

My hands are small. My will is strong.
The food I eat is food enough.
But as I age the days grow long,
The streets more narrow, violent, rough.
My hope is built on sterner stuff.

The help I offer is not quick.
I am no savior of the poor.
My father taught me what I know
And then he promptly closed the door
And gave to me the world, and more.

I can't keep up. My knees are weak.
I see the faster-moving light
That blazes over time and space
Emitting from each satellite
The speed that has undone the night.

My pleasures are the silence and
The quiet stretches, stark and still.
I value what is in my hand.
I do not need to pop a pill
To find my comfort or my thrill.

My world is paper, ink and time—
I value these commodities
More than the screen, and if I'm
Honest I would choose the trees
Over our vast technologies.

I slowly write my thoughts, my dreams
Which is responsibility.
But life is never as it seems.
Before *becoming* we must *be*
And grasp our mediocrity.

Origami

Imagine the perfect form and the way it will unfold
In a thousand wings or interstices of paper
How you will follow the instructions to create
Such beautiful lines

Then see yourself creating form of your own
Or cut on the margins anticipating that later
Your bright colors will dazzle in the sun's stare
And blossom into life

www.ingramcontent.com/pod-product-compliance
Lightning Source LLC
Chambersburg PA
CBHW071755090426
42737CB00012B/1835